What

Story by Brian and Jillian Cutting

A spider has a web to live in.
And what else?

A spider has ...
eight legs,
many eyes,
flies for dinner.

A bee has a hive to live in.
And what else?

A bee has ...
six legs,
wings to fly,
a stinger.

A frog has a pond to live in.
And what else?

A frog has ...
a croak for a voice,
feet for swimming,
a big jump.

A bird has a nest to live in.
And what else?

A bird has ...
feathers,
wings to fly,
a song to sing.

A bat has a cave to live in.
And what else?

A bat has ...
big ears,
feet to hang from in its cave,
sharp teeth.

A shark has an ocean to live in.
And what else?

A shark has ...
a fin,
rough skin,
big teeth.

Children have ...
eyes to see,
noses to smell,
ears to hear,
fingers to touch,
tongues to taste.

And what else?